WHAT · DO · WE · KNOW

ABOUT JUDAISM · ?

DOREEN FINE

MACDONALD YOUNG BOOKS

First published in 1995 and reprinted in 1998, by Macdonald Young Books

First published in paperback
by Macdonald Young Books in 1999

Macdonald Young Books
an imprint of Wayland Publishers Limited
61 Western Road
Hove
BN3 1JD

You can find Macdonald Young Books on the internet at
http://www.myb.co.uk

Designer and illustrator: Celia Hart
Commissioning editor: Debbie Fox
Editors: Caroline Arthur, Lesley Taylor
Picture research: Jane Taylor
Consultant: Laurie Rosenberg, Executive Director of Education, Board of
Deputies of British Jews

Photograph acknowledgements: Front and back cover: Stewart Weir; Andes
Press Agency, pp8, 41(b) (Carlos Reyes-Manzo); Architectural Association,
p21(b) (John Ross); MS Kennicott 1 Folio 305R, Bodleain Library Oxford;
Anat Rotem-Braun, Jerusalem, pp15(1), 29(t), 31(c); Werner Braun,
Jerusalem, p33(b); Bridgeman Art Library, pp13(t) Giraudon/ "Jacob's
Dream" by Ludovico Cardi da Cigoli (1559-1613), Musée des Beaux-Arts,
Nancy, 14 "Moses and the Tablets of the Law" by Hermensz
van Rijn Rembrandt (1606-69), Dahlem Staatliche Gemaldegalerie, Berlin,
34 "Saul Listening to David Playing the Harp" by Erasmus Quellinus
(1607-78), Museum of Fine Arts, Budapest, 41(t) "The Jewish Marriage"
by Ilex Bellers (20th century), Private Collection; British Library, Oriental &
India Office Collections, pp12, 13(c), 40; Camera Press, p31(t) (Y Braun);
Circa Photo Library, pp25(t), 43 (Barrie Searle); Kuperard Ltd, p20;
Hulton Deutsch Collection, p27 (br); Israeli Post Office, Philatetic Service,
p34(r); Henry Jacobs, p35(b); Michael Le Poer Trench, p13(b); Rony Oren,
The Animated Haggadah, Scopus Films (London) Ltd, p33(t) (Trevor
Clifford); Photo Researchers Inc, NY, p9; Zev Radovan, Jerusalem, pp27(bl),
31(b), 32, 37; Peter Sanders Photography, p36; Traditions Mail Order,
endpapers (Trevor Clifford), 39(t) from the original in the Israeli Museum
(Jeffrey Gendler); Stewart Weir, pp17(br), 23, 24, 25(b); 38, 39(b) Westhill
RE Centre, pp15(r), 16, 17(t), 30; Zefa Pictures, pp17(bl), 18, 19, 21(t), 22,
27, 28, 29(b), 35(t).

Printed by Wing King Tong, Hong Kong.

A CIP catalogue record for this book
is available from the British Library

ISBN: 0 7500 2799 1

Endpapers: This hand-painted silk Shabbat cloth shows
the seven foods harvested at Sukkot time:wheat, barley,
grapes, olives, pomegranates, dates and figs.
(by Yair Emanuel, Emanuel Studio, Jerusalem)

· CONTENTS ·

WHO·ARE·THE·JEWS?

Jews can be any nationality or colour, and they live in many countries around the world. The religion of Jews is Judaism, but you can be a Jew and not follow any religious beliefs or practices. Orthodox Jews believe that you are Jewish if your mother is Jewish, or if you become Jewish through a long course of study and practice. Some Progressive Jews believe that you are Jewish if either of your parents is Jewish, or if you accept the Jewish beliefs and way of life.

KIBBUTZ

Some Jews live isolated from any other Jews on remote farms, or in small towns and villages far away from centres of Jewish population. In Israel, many Jews live in communal farm villages. One type of farm village is known as a *kibbutz*. The kibbutz children live together, go to school together, work together and play together, as you can see in the photograph on the left. Their parents take turns at doing all the work in the kibbutz. This may be on the farm or in the houses, the kitchen or the laundry. They also take turns in managing the kibbutz.

GOLDERS GREEN, LONDON

Other Jews live in major towns and cities so that they can easily get to Jewish schools and shops which sell *kosher* food (see pages 16-17) and religious articles. In the photograph on the right, the people with the trays of goods from the kosher bakery are only a few steps away from two kosher restaurants. Nearby there are also Jewish bookshops, fish shops and grocery shops, and shops selling Jewish objects for the home. Orthodox Jews will not travel on *Shabbat* (Saturday), and so must live within walking distance of a synagogue.

Jews per 1000
people

■ Up to 800
Jews

□ Up to 100
Jews

▨ About 1 Jew

How the Jewish population is spread throughout the world

THE JEWISH WORLD

As you can see from the map above, the largest
number of Jews live in the USA, where there are
5.5 million Jews, followed by Israel, where there
are 4.5 million Jews. There are large communities
in Britain, France, the Russian Federation, South
America, Australia and South Africa. Most Jews live
in big cities. In New York there are about 1,450,000
Jews. In Britain there are about 300,000 Jews. About
200,000 of these live in London and the South East
of England. Most of the Jews from Iraq, Iran, the
Yemen and Ethiopia have moved to Israel, as have
many thousands from the Russian Federation.

 MODERN JEWS

Today, there are several different branches of
Judaism. Jews who still follow all the traditional
laws and customs are called Orthodox Jews. Within
Orthodox Judaism are the *Chasidic* movements,
such as *Lubavitch*. Non-Orthodox, or Progressive
Jews (those Jews who do not follow all the
traditions), also have different branches. In Britain,
there are *Masorti*, Reform and Liberal groups. In
the USA, there are Conservative, Reform and
Reconstructionist groups.

BROOKLYN, NEW YORK

Some Chasidic sects, particularly in the USA and
Israel, live in close communities, within a few
streets of their *Rebbe*, or leader. They are like a
village within a town or city. They will pray in their
own synagogue, send their children to their own
schools and wear distinctive clothing, as in the
photograph above.

TIMELINE

EVENTS IN JUDAISM

BCE = Before the Common Era = BC (term used by Christians)
CE = In the time of the Common Era = AD
JY = Jewish Year, counted from the Creation

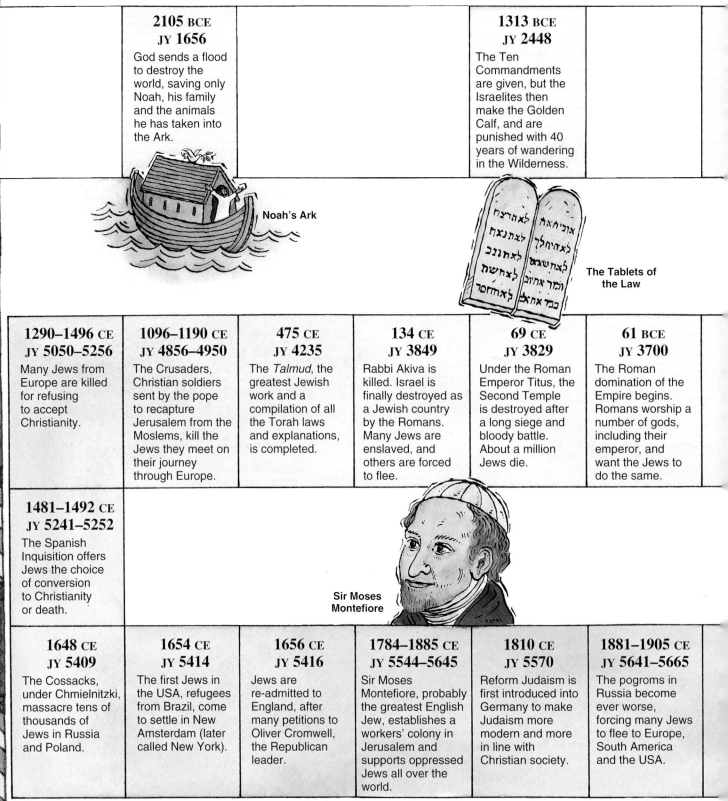

2105 BCE JY **1656** God sends a flood to destroy the world, saving only Noah, his family and the animals he has taken into the Ark.				**1313 BCE** JY **2448** The Ten Commandments are given, but the Israelites then make the Golden Calf, and are punished with 40 years of wandering in the Wilderness.	

Noah's Ark

The Tablets of the Law

1290–1496 CE JY **5050–5256** Many Jews from Europe are killed for refusing to accept Christianity.	**1096–1190 CE** JY **4856–4950** The Crusaders, Christian soldiers sent by the pope to recapture Jerusalem from the Moslems, kill the Jews they meet on their journey through Europe.	**475 CE** JY **4235** The *Talmud*, the greatest Jewish work and a compilation of all the Torah laws and explanations, is completed.	**134 CE** JY **3849** Rabbi Akiva is killed. Israel is finally destroyed as a Jewish country by the Romans. Many Jews are enslaved, and others are forced to flee.	**69 CE** JY **3829** Under the Roman Emperor Titus, the Second Temple is destroyed after a long siege and bloody battle. About a million Jews die.	**61 BCE** JY **3700** The Roman domination of the Empire begins. Romans worship a number of gods, including their emperor, and want the Jews to do the same.
1481–1492 CE JY **5241–5252** The Spanish Inquisition offers Jews the choice of conversion to Christianity or death.					

Sir Moses Montefiore

| **1648 CE**
JY **5409**
The Cossacks, under Chmielnitzki, massacre tens of thousands of Jews in Russia and Poland. | **1654 CE**
JY **5414**
The first Jews in the USA, refugees from Brazil, come to settle in New Amsterdam (later called New York). | **1656 CE**
JY **5416**
Jews are re-admitted to England, after many petitions to Oliver Cromwell, the Republican leader. | **1784–1885 CE**
JY **5544–5645**
Sir Moses Montefiore, probably the greatest English Jew, establishes a workers' colony in Jerusalem and supports oppressed Jews all over the world. | **1810 CE**
JY **5570**
Reform Judaism is first introduced into Germany to make Judaism more modern and more in line with Christian society. | **1881–1905 CE**
JY **5641–5665**
The pogroms in Russia become ever worse, forcing many Jews to flee to Europe, South America and the USA. |

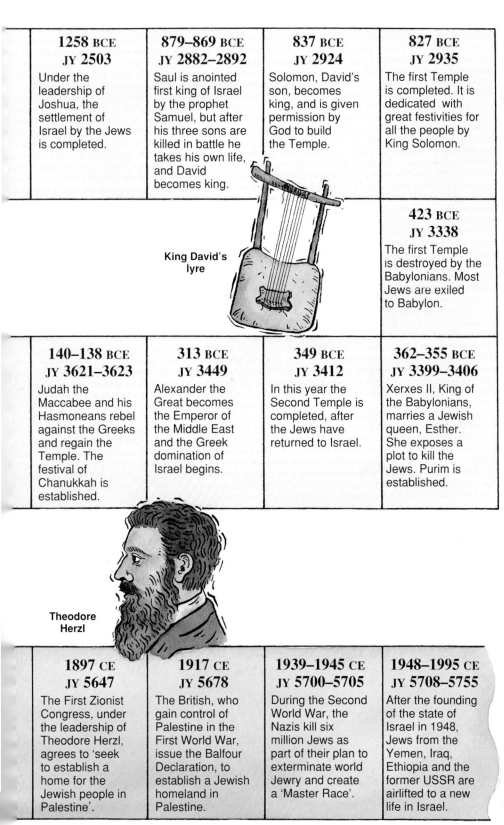

1258 BCE JY 2503	879–869 BCE JY 2882–2892	837 BCE JY 2924	827 BCE JY 2935
Under the leadership of Joshua, the settlement of Israel by the Jews is completed.	Saul is anointed first king of Israel by the prophet Samuel, but after his three sons are killed in battle he takes his own life, and David becomes king.	Solomon, David's son, becomes king, and is given permission by God to build the Temple.	The first Temple is completed. It is dedicated with great festivities for all the people by King Solomon.

King David's lyre

423 BCE
JY 3338

The first Temple is destroyed by the Babylonians. Most Jews are exiled to Babylon.

140–138 BCE JY 3621–3623	313 BCE JY 3449	349 BCE JY 3412	362–355 BCE JY 3399–3406
Judah the Maccabee and his Hasmoneans rebel against the Greeks and regain the Temple. The festival of Chanukkah is established.	Alexander the Great becomes the Emperor of the Middle East and the Greek domination of Israel begins.	In this year the Second Temple is completed, after the Jews have returned to Israel.	Xerxes II, King of the Babylonians, marries a Jewish queen, Esther. She exposes a plot to kill the Jews. Purim is established.

Theodore Herzl

1897 CE JY 5647	1917 CE JY 5678	1939–1945 CE JY 5700–5705	1948–1995 CE JY 5708–5755
The First Zionist Congress, under the leadership of Theodore Herzl, agrees to 'seek to establish a home for the Jewish people in Palestine'.	The British, who gain control of Palestine in the First World War, issue the Balfour Declaration, to establish a Jewish homeland in Palestine.	During the Second World War, the Nazis kill six million Jews as part of their plan to exterminate world Jewry and create a 'Master Race'.	After the founding of the state of Israel in 1948, Jews from the Yemen, Iraq, Ethiopia and the former USSR are airlifted to a new life in Israel.

THE STATE OF ISRAEL

From 69 CE, for over 1,800 years, Jews have prayed daily for the re-establishment of Israel as the Jewish homeland and for the rebuilding of the Temple.

After the Second World War, most Jews in the world had been either killed by the Nazis or forced to leave their countries, or were living in societies that either banned Judaism or persecuted them for being Jews.

In 1947, the United Nations, an organisation set up to establish world peace, recommended that Palestine be split into two separate states, Jewish and Arab. This was to give a safe haven to the displaced and unwanted Jews of the world. On 14 May 1948, the State of Israel was born.

Shield of David

MAGEN DAVID

The six-pointed star, the 'Shield of David', or the 'Seal of Solomon'as it was sometimes known, has been used as a particularly Jewish symbol since the late Middle Ages. However, it was used in Christian and Moslem culture as well as in earlier times. It was later adopted by the Zionist movement and for the national flag of Israel.

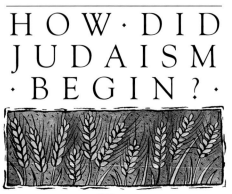

HOW·DID JUDAISM ·BEGIN?·

Jews believe that Judaism began when Abram, the father of the Jewish religion, began to worship one God instead of many idols as his father had done. According to the Torah, Abram was born in 1813 BCE and married Sarai. They set out on a journey led by God. Abram entered into a covenant or agreement with God. He promised to be faithful to God and to teach his laws to the world. To mark the covenant, Abram circumcised himself. God changed the names of the couple to Abraham and Sarah (the extra 'h' is a symbol for God). He promised that they would have a son. He said that their descendants would be as many as the stars in the sky and they would inherit the Land of Israel.

CANAANITE IDOLS

The people of the land of Canaan, where Abraham was born, worshipped idols – statues made of clay, stone or bronze. They believed that if they pleased the idols they would be granted their wishes, such as strength, victory in battle or a good harvest. To gain good fortune from the idols, people gave them offerings. Astarte, who is pictured below, was a well-known goddess. Baal was the most famous god.

Bronze statue of the goddess Astarte

ABRAHAM AND ISAAC

The painting above shows a famous scene from the story of Abraham. To test Abraham's character, God ordered Abraham to sacrifice Isaac, his favourite son, on Mount Moriah. Abraham obeyed, but God sent an angel to stop him. To show his thanks, Abraham looked around for a suitable offering to God. He found a ram caught in a bush. Can you see it in the painting?

12

The route the Israelites took when going from Egypt to Israel

Probable route of the Exodus ——

Another possible route ......

JACOB'S DREAM

Isaac and his son Jacob were the second and third founding fathers of Judaism. Jacob dreamed of a ladder going from Earth up to Heaven, with angels going up and down, as you can see in the painting above. Suddenly, he heard God speaking to him. God renewed the promise he made to Abraham and promised to look after Jacob, wherever he was. Jacob said he would be faithful to God. God then named Jacob 'Israel'.

JOSEPH

Joseph was Jacob's favourite son. Jacob gave him a special coat. Joseph was sold into slavery by his brothers. Later, he rose to power in Egypt because God told him the meaning of Pharaoh's – the king's – dreams. This popular story has been made into a modern musical. Here, Philip Schofield plays Joseph in *Joseph and the Amazing Technicolour Dreamcoat.*

THE EXODUS

After Joseph's death, a new pharaoh made the Israelites into slaves. He would not let them worship their own God, and drowned their baby boys in the River Nile. God appointed a new leader, Moses, and sent ten plagues to show Pharaoh his anger. After Pharaoh had let the Israelites leave Egypt, he chased after them. So as a punishment, God drowned Pharaoh's army in the Red Sea (pictured below).

THE CHILDREN OF ISRAEL

Abraham and Sarah had one son, Isaac. Isaac and Rebekkah had twins, Jacob and Esau. Jacob married four women: Leah and Rachel, and their maids, Bilhah and Zilpah. Jacob's sons became the fathers of the Twelve Tribes of Israel. Leah's sons were Reuben, Simeon, Levi, Judah, Issachar and Zebulun. Rachel's sons were Joseph and Benjamin. Zilpah's sons were Gad and Asher, and Bilhah's were Dan and Naphtali.

WHAT·DO·JEWS·BELIEVE?

There is a wide range of Jewish beliefs. Progressive Jews believe that being Jewish gives them a common culture, while Orthodox Jews try to keep all the laws and customs laid down over the centuries. The basic Jewish religious belief is in the existence of one, eternal, invisible God. The Jews also believe they were chosen to receive God's *Torah* – the first part of the *Tenakh* (the Jewish bible). They believe that by looking at its many meanings, and by living according to its laws, they can spread justice throughout the world. At the right time, they believe that the Messiah will come to bring this perfect world. Reward for good deeds will largely be granted in the World to Come (Heaven).

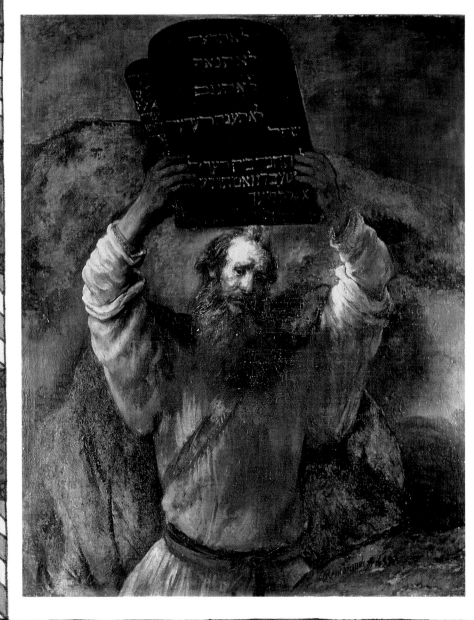

THE TABLETS OF THE LAW

Jews believe that seven weeks after the Israelites left Egypt, God chose them to receive the Torah. Moses climbed Mount Sinai to hear the Torah and bring the Commandments back to the people, carved into stone tablets. In this painting, Moses is holding the second tablet in front, which shows Commandments six to ten. The stone tablets were kept in a special gold box – the Ark – inside a magnificent tent – the Tabernacle – in the Wilderness.

THE TEN COMMANDMENTS

1 I am the Lord your God.
2 You shall not have any other gods.
3 You shall not take a false oath in My name.
4 Remember the Sabbath Day and to keep it holy.
5 Honour your father and mother.
6 Do not murder.
7 Do not take another's wife or husband.
8 Do not steal.
9 Do not tell lies.
10 Do not be jealous.

THE SIX DAYS OF CREATION

First Day

Second Day

The Jews believe that on the first day of the Creation of the World, God made night and day. Earth and Heaven were created on the second day, and seas and land and everything that grows from the ground on the third day. On the fourth day, the Sun, Moon and stars were created, and on the fifth day, the fish and birds. On the sixth day, God made all land animals and, finally, people.

Sixth Day

Fifth Day

Third Day

Fourth Day

ORTHODOX JEWS

Many Jews carry out even everyday activities in special ways, believing that this brings them closer to God. The men in the photograph are immersing cooking pots in water in preparation for the Passover. Water is a symbol for purity in Judaism and is used in other ceremonies. People sometimes immerse themselves in 'living water' – rain, river or sea water – in a special pool called a *mikveh*. A convert to Judaism uses the mikveh as a symbol to show re-birth as a Jew. The long side-curls and beards worn by the men on the left show their interpretation of certain laws concerning cutting hair.

WOMAN RABBI

Progressive Jews believe that laws can be changed to suit modern times. One recent change states that men and women should be equal in every area of Jewish practice. Rabbi Tabick is one of the first women rabbis (or religious leaders) in Britain. She can carry out all the religious duties in her synagogue.

·HOW·DO· ·JEWISH· FAMILIES ·LIVE?·

Family life, which is so important in Judaism, is centred around Shabbat, festivals and family meals. It includes learning, singing and conversation. Eating kosher food and the separation of meat and milk foods are important features of Jewish living. Principles of Jewish family behaviour include: honouring your parents, helping those less able than yourself, respecting old people, hospitality to strangers, visiting the sick, and not gossiping or telling lies about people. Jewish education begins in the home. Children learn by example and are helped to carry out Jewish rituals from childhood.

MEZUZAH

Every Jewish home should have a *mezuzah* fixed to the frame of most doors in the house. The mezuzah is a handwritten parchment scroll with the words of the *Shema* prayer – the most important Jewish prayer. It commands Jews to fix a mezuzah to their doorposts. Some families have a special celebration when they move to a new house and fix the mezuzah to the front door. Usually the mezuzah is rolled up inside a beautiful case, like the one in the drawing.

Mezuzah

CHARITY BOX

Giving charity is a basic Jewish belief and many Jewish homes have at least one charity box. Children are often given money to put in the box on Friday, in honour of Shabbat. Adults in the family also put in money regularly. The money from the box on the right went to buy clothes for people who had none.

KOSHER FOOD GUIDE

Many Jewish families use a food guide to help make sure that any foods they buy or eat outside the home are strictly kosher. Some guides, like the one in the picture, give advice about medicines and kosher cooking as well.

Kosher food guide

JEWISH FOOD GUIDE

The London Beth Din Kosher Guide
Shabbat/Festival Calendar
Recipes

Charity box

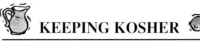 KEEPING KOSHER

The rules for kosher animals, birds and fish come directly from the Torah.

Kosher fish include:
plaice, salmon, sardines, trout, herring, sole and cod.

Kosher animals include:
cows, sheep, goats and deer.

Kosher birds include:
chickens, ducks, geese and turkeys.

Animals and birds must be killed by a special method, called *Shechitah*.

A KOSHER KITCHEN

According to the rules of *kashrut* – kosher eating – milk and all other dairy products, such as cheese, may not be cooked or eaten with meat. In the kosher kitchen above, meat meals are cooked and washed up with red equipment, and foods containing milk products with blue equipment. There are even separate sinks and dishwashers for milk and meat equipment.

WASHING BEFORE A MEAL

The picture above shows a young girl being taught the correct way to wash her hands before a meal. Jewish children begin taking part in rituals and ceremonies from the age of three and many aspects of the Jewish way of life are learnt in the home.

THE FAMILY

Jews consider large families to be a blessing. In fact, all Jews are like one large family and all Jews feel responsible for each other. A family outing, as in the photograph, is one way of being together. Many Jewish ceremonies and rituals involve not only parents but children and other members of the family, such as grandparents.

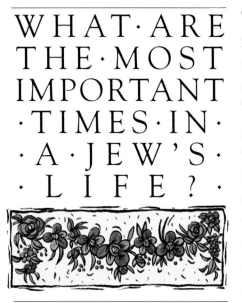

WHAT·ARE THE·MOST IMPORTANT ·TIMES·IN· ·A·JEW'S· ·LIFE?·

The four most important stages in Jewish life are birth, reaching adulthood, marriage and death. All of these are marked by religious ceremonies, some of which are unchanged since they were first commanded in the Torah. During these ceremonies the family and community say thankyou to God. They also say that they believe in God and accept God's will. All Jewish ceremonies, such as circumcision and naming ceremonies for boys, naming ceremonies for girls, weddings, deaths and memorial services, enable people to share their happiness and sorrow. They can carry out religious duties and feel part of a warm and caring community.

JEWISH NAMES

As well as a first name and a surname, such as Claire Jones, Jews also have a Jewish name. In a Jewish name, people are known by their first names, followed by 'son of' or 'daughter of' their parents' first names. Sometimes only the father's name is used and sometimes only the mother's. Some Jews use both parents' names at all times. So if a boy's first name is David, his mother is Ruth and his father is Aaron, he is David ben (son of) Aaron, or David ben Ruth, or David ben Aaron and Ruth. David's sister, Esther, would be Esther bat (daughter of) Aaron, or Esther bat Ruth, or Esther bat Aaron and Ruth.

CIRCUMCISION AND NAMING

When he is eight days old, a boy is circumcised. This is to show his entry into the covenant of Abraham. He is given his Jewish name and everyone prays that he should be blessed with Torah study, marriage and good deeds.

A girl may be named by her father in a synagogue immediately after birth, or at a baby-naming ceremony.

Cushion used at a circumcision ceremony

BAR MITZVAH

When a boy reaches 13, he becomes *Bar Mitzvah*. This means that he takes on all the religious and legal obligations of an adult. For example, he should wear *tefillin* – two small black leather boxes with leather straps – each weekday morning, as the boy in the photograph on the left is learning to do. Bar Mitzvah is celebrated in many communities by calling a boy up to the Torah reading on Shabbat morning, which is an adult privilege. Usually the Bar Mitzvah will read part or all of the morning's Torah reading and say the blessings for the first time. In celebration, the family often gives a *kiddush* – a reception – in the synagogue and a festive meal at home.

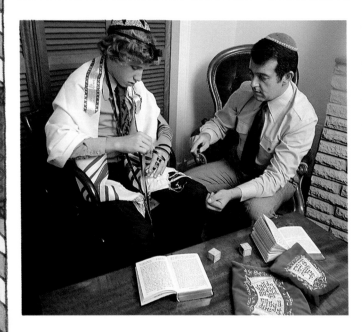

BAT MITZVAH

A 12-year-old girl celebrates becoming *Bat Mitzvah*. In Progressive communities, she may learn to read from the Torah, as in the photograph on the right. Orthodox girls may celebrate their Bat Mitzvah in the synagogue, at home, at school, or in a Sunday afternoon ceremony.

MARRIAGE

Jewish weddings, more than any other Jewish ceremony, vary around the world. They can be informal, outdoor ceremonies, or very formal synagogue ceremonies as shown in the photograph below. All weddings have the *chuppah* – a canopy – which is a symbol for the couple's new home, and a veil is worn over the bride's face. A glass is broken by the groom. This is to remember the destruction of the two Temples.

Memorial candle

Ceremonial wedding ring

DEATH AND MOURNING

The bodies of Orthodox Jews are always buried, but some Progressive Jews allow cremation. After the funeral, the parents, husband or wife, sisters, brothers or children of the dead person observe the *shivah* – a seven-day mourning period. They sit on low chairs all day, while family and friends visit to pray with them, comfort them and bring them food. On the anniversary of the death, every year, a memorial candle is lit and special prayers are said.

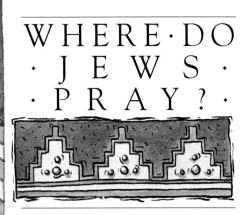

WHERE·DO ·JEWS· ·PRAY?·

Jews pray anywhere and everywhere! Every action and occasion is an opportunity for them to pray. Whenever Jews eat or drink, put on new clothes, hear bad news, go to bed or get up, there is a suitable blessing to say. If Jews go on a long journey, there is a prayer to say. If they are not sure what prayer to say, in a place where something terrible has happened, or where something wonderful has happened, they are encouraged to make up their own prayers. In the synagogue, there are prayers to say for every occasion.

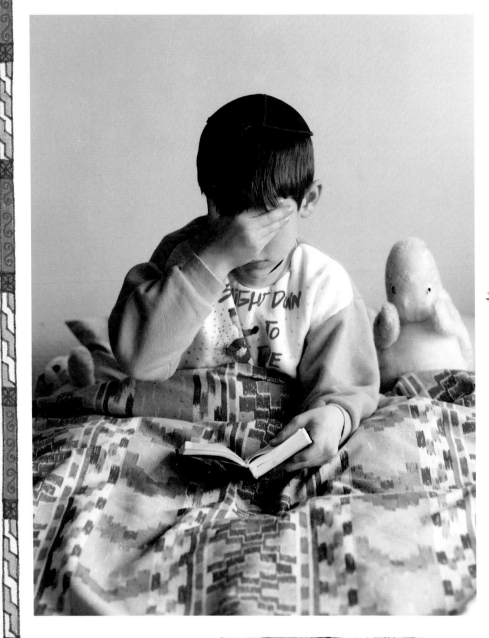

PRAYING IN BED

This boy in the photograph is saying the bedtime prayers. He is covering his eyes to help him concentrate on the Shema prayer. He will also ask God and the most important angels, the archangels Michael, Gabriel, Uriel and Raphael, to guard him while he sleeps.

TIMES FOR PRAYER

Some Jewish prayers, such as the morning, afternoon and evening prayers, need to be said at fixed times, wherever you are. Orthodox Jewish men of 13 years and over are always supposed to say these prayers. Women traditionally had to look after the home and children and could not be expected to stop everything to pray. Therefore there are fewer prayers that they must say. Many Progressive Jews only say these prayers when they are in the synagogue, on Shabbat or during the festivals.

THE SYNAGOGUE IN DJERBA

Jews have been praying in synagogues since the time of the first Temple (827 BCE). This synagogue in Tunisia is very old. It is in the style of Arab buildings. The men are praying at tables and benches and are wearing the traditional clothes of Jews of Arab lands, such as the red hat called a *fez*.

ORTHODOX AND PROGRESSIVE SYNAGOGUES

The main difference between an Orthodox and a Progressive synagogue is that in Progressive synagogues men and women sit together for prayer and in Orthodox synagogues they are separated. Sometimes women sit behind a screen at the same level as the men; sometimes they sit upstairs in a balcony. Below are examples of the inside of an Orthodox synagogue and an American Progressive synagogue.

Orthodox synagogue

Progressive synagogue

THE BETH SHALOM SYNAGOGUE

This spectacular synagogue was designed by the famous architect Frank Lloyd Wright in 1959. It was built for the congregation at Elkins Park, Philadelphia, USA. Modern synagogues like this are a sign that Judaism is thriving in the 20th century. The synagogue is the centre of a Jewish community. A modern synagogue is not only a place of prayer and study, but also houses social, leisure and welfare services for members, friends and visitors.

HOW·DO ·JEWS· ·PRAY?·

From about the age of three, Jews are encouraged to bring God into all activities by saying short prayers such as *berachot* – blessings – which are for every occasion. Then there are set prayer services, which Orthodox Jewish men are obliged to say three times each day, in Hebrew. Prayers are silent, chanted aloud, or sung. Many Progressive Jews have shortened these, and say them only in the synagogue on Friday nights, Shabbat mornings and special occasions. They pray in a mixture of Hebrew and the local language. Normally, Jews pray sitting or standing, though some prayers should be said when in bed, like the bedtime Shema.

PRAYING IN A SYNAGOGUE

Prayers in the synagogue can be led by the Rabbi, the Cantor – who is a professional prayer leader – or an ordinary person. In an Orthodox synagogue, prayers can be led only by men, or boys of thirteen years or over. In the photograph above, you can see the Cantor, who has his back to the congregation and is singing a special prayer while the Torah scrolls are taken out of the Holy Ark. The Rabbi is on the far right of the photograph. In many Progressive synagogues, prayers can also be led by women, and men and women sit together.

SAYING THE MORNING SERVICE

In the photograph on the right, an Orthodox Jewish man is saying the weekday morning service. He is wearing a small skull cap, called a *yarmulke* or *kippah*; a prayer shawl, called a *tallit*, and *tefillin*. The two boxes of the tefillin are worn on the head and next to the heart, and they contain holy prayers. This is to remind the wearer each day of the important message of the Shema prayer. Do you think that wearing special clothes and religious symbols helps people when they pray?

 ## THE SHEMA PRAYER

Listen Israel, the Lord is our God, the Lord is one. Let the name of his magnificent kingdom be blessed for ever and ever.

You shall love the Lord your God with all your heart, with all your soul and with everything you have. Let these words, which I command you today, be on your heart. Teach them carefully to your children. Speak of them when you are sitting at home and when you are travelling, when you go to bed and when you get up. Tie them on your arm as a sign and as tefillin between your eyes. Write them on the doorposts of your house and on your gateposts.

BLESSING THE CHILDREN

Before the meal on Fridays and on festival evenings, parents bless their children, praying that God will help them and look after them. Girls are blessed with the good qualities of the 'Four Mothers' of the Jewish people – Sarah, Rebekkah, Rachel and Leah. Boys are blessed with Jacob's blessing for his grandsons, Ephraim and Menasseh.

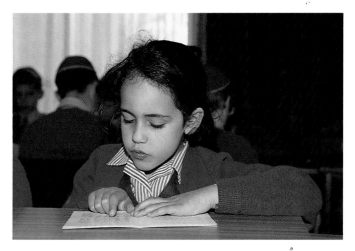

PRAYING AT MEALTIMES

Before lunch, these children in a Jewish school wash their hands in a special way, as shown in the photograph on page 17. They say one short blessing. They then say another blessing, after which they eat a piece of bread and then their meal. After lunch, as in this photograph, the children say and sing *Birkat Hamazon* – the Blessings after Meals – from special books that are written in Hebrew.

WHAT·DO ·JEWS· ·DO·ON· SHABBAT?

On Friday night, a little before sunset, Shabbat, the day of rest, begins. It lasts until after dark on Saturday night. Many Jews put aside all weekday activities and worries. They prepare their homes as if for a royal visitor – the Shabbat Queen – and put on their best clothes. They also light candles, and serve the best food they can afford at a beautifully set table. Often guests are invited to share meals, songs, stories, prayers and Torah learning. Attending the synagogue, visits to friends, walks and study activities all add to the spirit of the day.

Havdalah candle

LIGHTING CANDLES

Shabbat enters the Jewish home with the lighting of at least two candles that symbolise joy and holiness, and the saying of a blessing. Some families add another candle for each child. As you can see in the photograph, whoever lights the candles – often mothers and daughters – welcomes in Shabbat with a gesture over the candles; they then cover their eyes to say the blessing.

ACTIVITIES FORBIDDEN ON SHABBAT

There were 39 types of activity that were carried out when building the Tabernacle in the Wilderness, but which had to stop on Shabbat, to make it a day of complete rest. Today, this same law means that Orthodox Jews don't do any of the following once Shabbat has begun:

cook; light a fire; switch on electrical equipment; write; watch television; play musical instruments; travel in a car, bus, boat, train or aeroplane, or ride a bicycle or motorbike. In order to follow the law, food, light and heat are all prepared before Shabbat to last the whole day.

FOOD FOR SHABBAT

At dinner on Friday night and Shabbat lunch, the meal starts with blessings over wine and two *challot* – special loaves of bread. Jews were often very poor and many of the traditional recipes were clever ways of making a little meat or fish feed a lot of people! Examples are liver, chopped with egg and onion, and *gefilte* fish (a type of fishcake). *Cholent*, or *hamim,* is meat stewed with onions, potatoes and beans on a low heat over Friday night and Shabbat morning so that there will be a hot meal for lunch. Chicken soup and chicken are also enjoyed every week in many Jewish homes.

Cholent
(hamim)

Chopped
herring

Gefilte fish

Chopped
liver

Challot

READING THE TORAH

Each Shabbat is known by the name of that week's Torah reading. The Torah reading is the central part of the morning service. The Torah scroll, the most holy object in Judaism, is taken to the *bimah* – the reading desk on the stage – in a stately procession. Reading from the Torah, as the rabbi in the photograph on the right is doing, is a special skill. It is a great honour to read it, or to be called to stand on the bimah to hear a section read.

HAVDALAH

Just as the arrival of Shabbat is celebrated, so is its departure, with prayer and ceremony. When three stars can be seen in the sky, Shabbat is over for another week and *Havdalah* (the separation) is celebrated. Havdalah, which separates the holiness of Shabbat from the ordinariness of the weekday, is performed with blessings over wine, spices and a plaited candle, as the photograph on the left shows. Children eagerly await their turn to hold the candle and to sniff the sweet-smelling spices.

·HOW·DOES· THE·JEWISH CALENDAR ·WORK?·

The Jewish calendar has 12 months which run according to the Moon, rather than the Sun, as the civil calendar does. Each Jewish month has either 29 or 30 days and every Jewish year is about 11 days shorter than a civil year. The Jewish calendar must keep up with the civil year, or all the festivals would eventually end up in the wrong seasons. (Jewish festivals are celebrated on fixed dates.) To do this, the calendar has leap years, with an extra month of Adar in January–February. The normal month of Adar (February–March) is then called Adar 2. There are seven leap years every 19 years. There is a celebration, *Rosh Chodesh*, for the beginning of each month.

THE JEWISH CALENDAR

Tishrei (September–October)
Rosh Hashanah (2 days)
Yom Kippur (1 day)
Sukkot (7 days)
Shemini Atzeret (1day)
Simchat Torah (1 day)

Cheshvan (October–November)
There are no festivals in Cheshvan.
It is sometimes known as MarCheshvan or 'bitter Cheshvan'
for this reason.

Kislev (November–December)   Chanukkah (8 days)

Tevet (December–January)   Chanukkah

Shevat (January–February)   Tu Bishvat (1 day)
(New Year for Trees)

Adar (February–March)   Purim (1 day)

Nisan (March–April)   Pesach (7–8 days)
Yom HaSho'ah (1 day)

Iyyar (April–May)   Yom Ha'Atsma'ut (1 day)
(Israel's Independence Day)
Lag baOmer (1 day)

Sivan (May–June)   Shavuot (1–2 days)

Tammuz (June–July)   Fast of Tammuz

Av (July–August)   Tishah b'Av (1 day)
(Day of Mourning)

Elul (August–September)   Preparations for
Rosh Hashanah

There are no festivals in Elul.

ROSH HASHANAH AND YOM KIPPUR

The Jewish New Year, *Rosh Hashanah*, is on 1 and 2 Tishrei (September-October). *Yom Kippur*, a 25-hour fast and the most solemn festival, is on 10 Tishrei. The first ten days of Tishrei, which include these two festivals, are known as the Ten Days of Penitence. During this period, Jews apologise to people and to God for wrongdoings. They pray for forgiveness and a new start in life. The *shofar* or ram's horn is blown to wake up the conscience, as in the photograph on the left. People send each other New Year cards, wishing a happy, healthy and sweet year. Some wear white clothes and use white material for all cloths and hangings in the synagogue, as a symbol of purity and newness. Bread and apple are dipped in honey, to symbolise sweetness, and honey cake is a traditional treat.

YOM HA'ATSMA'UT

Israel's Independence Day is the only festival that has been added to the calendar for hundreds of years. The State of Israel was created by the United Nations on 14 May 1948 CE. In Israel this date is celebrated as a national holiday, and it is a festival in Jewish communities throughout the world. Celebrations include services of thanksgiving and parties with Israeli folksinging.

YOM HASHO'AH

On 27 *Nisan*, Jews all over the world hold ceremonies honouring the memory of the six million Jews killed by the Nazis, before and during the Second World War, from 1939 to 1945 CE. Many Jewish families and whole towns of Jews were completely destroyed. One of the most famous victims was Anne Frank photographed above. Her diary has been read by thousands of people.

· W H A T · ARE · THE · THREE · PILGRIM · FESTIVALS?

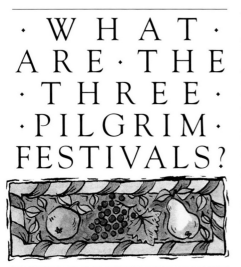

When the Temple was standing, Jews made a pilgrimage to Jerusalem to make offerings on the three festivals of *Pesach*, *Shavuot* and *Sukkot*. Jews who lived outside Israel had to sell part of their crops and send the money to buy offerings and to help in the upkeep of the Temple and the priests. Pesach, or Passover, is the festival that celebrates the Exodus from Egypt. A lamb was offered at the Temple. At Shavuot, some of the first produce of each harvest had to be offered at the Temple. Sukkot is the festival of the end of the harvest. Harvest offerings were made at the Temple. Now there is no Temple, Jews celebrate these festivals at home and in the synagogue.

PESACH

This beautiful plate is an example of those that are used at Pesach Seder services in Jewish homes. The pictures around the rim are the Ten Plagues suffered by the Egyptians. The bone is a symbol of the Pesach lamb, and the burnt egg symbolises the festival offering. Both were offered at the Temple. Next to the bone is bitter horseradish, symbolising the bitter life under the Egyptians. Next to the egg is *charoset*, a spicy nut mixture which symbolises the mortar for building the pyramids. Below that is salt-water, for the tears of the Israelites, and lastly green vegetables. All are eaten, or talked about, in a special order. One of the most important ingredients of the service is *matzah* or unleavened bread. This was the bread of the poor people. The Israelites ate this in Egypt and took it with them when they left.

SHAVUOT

Shavuot is exactly seven weeks after Pesach. It commemorates the giving of the Torah. It is also the Festival of the First Fruits, which the Israeli kibbutz children in the photograph are celebrating. These seven weeks are known as the *Omer*. A 'countdown', looking forward to Shavuot, is made each night. Synagogues are decorated with flowers as a reminder that Mount Sinai was decorated by God in the same way for this miraculous occasion. It is customary to eat dairy foods, such as cheesecake.

SUKKOT

At Sukkot all over the world Jews build temporary huts. They eat in them, as the family in the photograph below is doing. The *sukkah*, or hut, is to remind them of the fragile dwellings in the Wilderness, which were protected by God. It also reminds them of the huts that the farmers moved into at harvest time to be near their crops. The roof is made of cut branches and must be open to the sky. This family in Israel has lined the walls and hung up decorations. What have they made the walls from?

THE SUKKOT HARVEST

There are seven types of food that were harvested at Sukkot time in Israel. Many Jews hang samples of each type of food from the ceiling of the sukkah to symbolise the harvest. These foods were: wheat, barley, grapes, olives, pomegranates, dates and figs. Can you see any in the photograph below?

THE LULAV AND ETROG

The *lulav*, or palm frond, is bound in a bundle, together with willow and myrtle branches. The *etrog*, a lemon-like citrus fruit, is used with this bundle in special blessings and ceremonies held during Sukkot. One tradition says that the palm frond represents the spine, the myrtle leaves are the eyes, the willow leaves the mouth, and the etrog the heart. This represents the worship of God with the whole body.

Lulav

Etrog

Unlike Rosh Hashanah, Yom Kippur and the Pilgrim Festivals, several festivals are not mentioned in the Torah, but they have existed for hundreds of years. *Purim* and *Chanukkah* began as permanent reminders of miraculous events in which God saved or helped the Jews against enormous odds. These festivals, and *Tu Bishvat*, the New Year for Trees, were recorded in the *Talmud* (the encyclopedia of Torah laws) before the end of the fifth century CE. *Simchat Torah*, the Festival of Rejoicing in the Torah, was introduced several hundred years later.

SIMCHAT TORAH

Reading and learning Jewish texts is one of the most important Jewish activities. It is customary to celebrate finishing the study of any Jewish book. The celebration for completing the annual cycle of reading the Torah is a joyous event. All the Torah scrolls are taken out of the Holy Ark. Members of the community are given the honour of dancing with the scrolls and circling the synagogue in processions, as in the photograph above.

THE TORAH

The Torah consists of five books – the Five Books of Moses. Each of these books is divided into sections, known as *sidrot*. The first book is divided into 12, the second book into 11, the third into 10, the fourth into 10 and the fifth into 11, making 54 sidrot altogether. At least one section is read every Shabbat so that the whole cycle of readings is completed every year.

CHANUKKAH

Chanukkah celebrates the capture of the Temple from the Greeks and its re-dedication by the Maccabees, a Jewish guerrilla group. There was enough holy oil for the ever-burning *menorah* – the seven-branched candlestick – for only one day, but it lasted eight days, until more oil could be prepared. This is celebrated by lighting an extra light each night in an eight-branched menorah. Jews also eat foods cooked in oil.

Olive oil

Potato latkes   **Doughnuts**

TU BISHVAT

The New Year for Trees has been an important date since Talmudic times. It is often marked by planting new trees, especially those varieties mentioned in the *Tenakh* – the Jewish bible. The photograph on the right shows some Israeli girl soldiers fulfilling their army service by working on national agricultural projects. As the date is 15 *Shevat*, Jews have the custom of eating fifteen different types of fruit to mark the day.

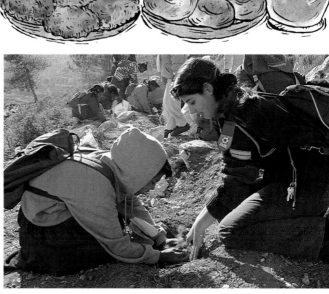

PURIM

Megillat Esther, the story of Purim, is read from a parchment scroll, with much noise being made to blot out the name of Haman, the villain. As you can see in the photograph, people of all ages dress up and enjoy Purim feasts. Friends exchange gifts of food and food gifts are given to the poor. Traditional foods include Purim loaves and *Hamantaschen,* or Haman's ears. These are triangular-shaped pastries, filled with jam or sweetened poppyseed paste.

Wine

Hamantaschen

WHAT·ARE THE·JEWS' ·HOLY· ·BOOKS?·

The holiest Jewish book is the Torah scroll, a parchment scroll on which the Five Books of Moses are handwritten. The Torah is the first part of the *Tenakh*. The second part is the *Nevi'im* – the books of the Prophets. The third part is the *Ketuvim* – all the other books of the Jewish bible, which include Psalms, Proverbs and the five *Megillot* (special stories or poems), each of which is associated with a festival. Prayerbooks and the books of the *Talmud* (dictated at Sinai, but not written down for centuries) are other Jewish holy books.

TORAH

The Torah scroll is wound on two wooden rollers. It is either encased in a richly embroidered cover and decorated with silver bells and crowns, or (as in the photograph on the left) mounted in a magnificent wooden case. The case is highly decorated, both inside and out, and is traditional for Oriental Jews. The case stands upright on the reading desk for the Torah to be read.

THE HEBREW ALPHABET

Hebrew is the language of the *Tenakh* and is a holy language. Each letter also represents a number. The Hebrew which is spoken in Israel today is similar to the Hebrew of the Torah. The *Talmud* is written in Aramaic. This was the everyday language of the Jews of Palestine and Babylon at the time it was written. Aramaic is written in Hebrew characters, which you can see below.

◄— read from right to left

◄— Vowels

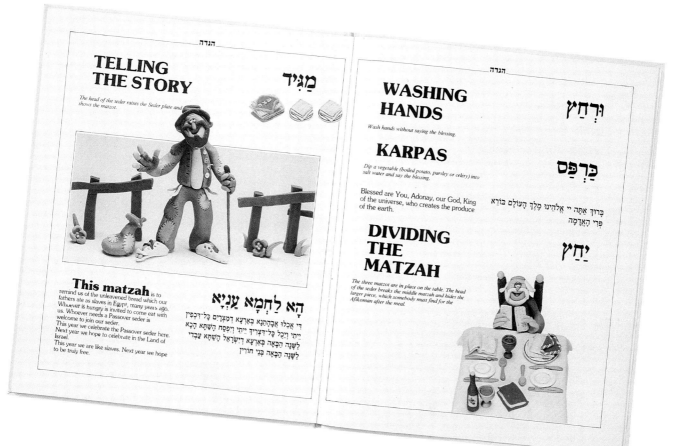

THE HAGGADAH

The *Haggadah* contains the prayers, service and songs for the Passover Seder. It is one of the earliest Jewish books and there are still some copies in existence today that are more than 500 years old. Although every Haggadah contains the same basic contents, many have extra stories and songs and contain extra Jewish history. In many families, each member has his or her own Haggadah. Each person adds something to the service from this book. The modern Haggadah in the photograph above is designed for children, with attractive and colourful pictures, many featuring clay models.

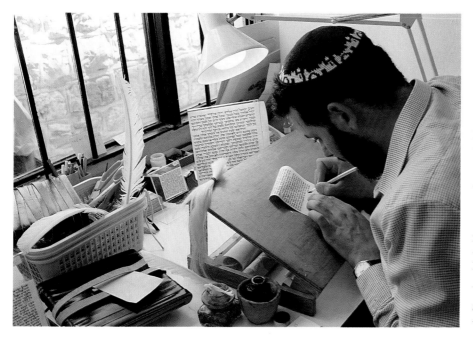

THE SCRIBE

Torah scrolls and the scroll inside the mezuzah must be handwritten with a quill pen, on specially prepared parchment, with ink made to an ancient recipe. Writing a Torah scroll takes about a year. There are strict rules to follow as to how every word is written and spaced. The scribe is highly skilled and knows all the religious requirements of his art. In the photograph on the left, a scribe is writing a mezuzah scroll, with the words of the Shema prayer. Look at all his tools. Can you see in which direction the writing goes?

· WHO · ARE·THE· JEWISH LEADERS?

From earliest times, Jewish leaders are believed by Jews to be men and women chosen by God as prophets to lead and teach the people. The Twelve Tribes were headed by princes. Later, when the Israelites were settled in Israel, they also had judges, kings and rabbis as leaders. Since the destruction of the Second Temple and the collapse of Israel as a country (until it was reinstated in 1948), rabbis have been the religious leaders. In Orthodox Judaism only male rabbis are allowed, but there are now a number of Progressive women rabbis.

SAUL AND DAVID

Saul was the first king of Israel. He used to have fits of depression and was often comforted by the harp music of a young man called David (his son Jonathan's best friend) as you can see in the painting. Later, Saul learned that David would succeed him as king, and tried to kill David, but Jonathan saved him. King David is famous for composing many psalms and making Jerusalem his capital.

PROPHETS

There were many prophets who were leaders, including Moses, Aaron, Miriam and Joshua. They believed totally in God's justice, and constantly tried to persuade the Jewish people to behave decently amongst themselves and with other people. Famous prophets include: Samuel, Elijah, Jeremiah, Hosea, Jonah and Deborah, one of the few female leaders in the Tenakh.

MAIMONIDES

Maimonides, shown on the right, was also known as Rabbi Moses ben Maimon, or Rambam. He was born in the 12th century CE. He was one of the greatest medieval rabbis. His books are still studied today. Born in Spain, Maimonides later moved to Egypt to escape religious persecution and took up medicine. He became court physician, as well as a community leader, and continued to study Jewish law and philosophy.

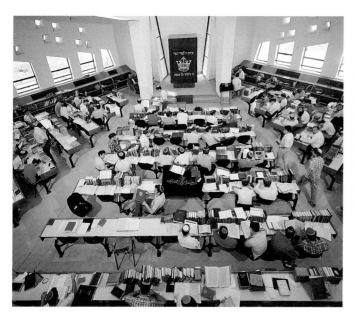

TRAINING TO BE A RABBI

Many young men go to a *yeshiva* – the college for rabbis – when they leave school. They study the holy books for up to 18 hours a day, as in the photograph on the left. Qualification for a rabbi is given only after years of study and written and oral examinations. Nowadays, many Orthodox rabbis and all Progressive rabbis study at university for degrees. Modern rabbis are also trained in public speaking, counselling (advice) and a range of other skills needed for the modern world.

A Sephardi rabbi

THE RABBI AS LEADER

In the photograph above, the Chief Rabbi of the United Synagogues of Britain, Dr Jonathan Sacks, presents a certificate of rabbinic ordination to a young graduate, Rabbi Broder. Rabbi Dr Sacks is the leader of the largest group of Jews in Britain. In Israel, there are two chief rabbis, one for the *Ashkenazi* community (Western and European Jews),

and one for the *Sephardi* community (Spanish, Portuguese and Oriental Jews). There are chief rabbis in other countries, such as France and Italy, but not in the USA. Many Progressive communities choose a rabbi to be leader or spokesperson for a number of years.

WHICH·ARE THE·JEWS' · HOLY · ·PLACES?·

The holiest place in Judaism was the Temple, which was built on Mount Moriah in Jerusalem. It was destroyed by the Greeks. The second Temple was built on the same site, but destroyed by the Romans. Another holy place in Jerusalem is the Mount of Olives, a holy Jewish burial site. Although the burial places of Moses, Aaron and Miriam are not known, the burial sites of other leaders are places for pilgrimage and prayer. These include David's tomb, the Cave of Machpelah and the tombs of many famous rabbis. The tombs of Rabbi Maimonides and Rabbi Akiva, for example, are in Tiberias.

THE WESTERN WALL

The only remaining part of both Temples is the Western Wall, sometimes known as the Wailing Wall, in Jerusalem. Jewish and non-Jewish people from all over the world visit at all hours of the day and night, on weekdays, Shabbat and Jewish holidays. They push little pieces of paper with prayers and requests in between the holy stones of the Wall. They come to pray alone or with a group, and to feel close to God. As you can see in the photograph above, the area directly in front of the Wall is arranged so that men and women pray separately, divided by a screen.

MOUNT OF OLIVES

The Mount of Olives, shown above, is the holiest Jewish burial site. This is because traditionally it is the route that the Messiah will take into Jerusalem when he comes to bring all the dead back to life. The people buried on the Mount of Olives will be the first to follow him into the Eternal Kingdom of God.

 ## CAVE OF MACHPELAH

The Cave of Machpelah, in Hebron, is the burial cave bought by Abraham. It is traditionally the burial place of Adam and Eve, Abraham and Sarah, Isaac and Rebekkah, and Jacob and Leah. Rachel, Jacob's favourite wife, was buried outside the original border of Israel, in Bethlehem.

JERUSALEM

Jerusalem is the holiest Jewish city on Earth, as it was the site of the two Temples for hundreds of years. However, it is also holy to Moslems and Christians. Therefore, it is important that people of all faiths can worship there freely. Jerusalem was set up as the capital of King David about 3,000 years ago, and has been captured by many rulers over the centuries. They wanted it to be only for members of their own faith. The Crusades (religious wars) began in 1096 CE because the Pope wanted to capture Jerusalem from the Moslems.

Sites of Jewish holy places

· W H A T · · A R E · T H E · J E W I S H R I T U A L O B J E C T S ?

Judaism is a way of life and almost every Jewish activity has a special religious object associated with it. This may be a simple jug for hand-washing in the home, or the most ornate Torah scroll in the synagogue. Tradition encourages Jewish people to carry out religious duties willingly and with joy. Therefore, ritual objects are made of the best materials the owner can afford and decorated lovingly with embroidery and ornaments. If a Jew can afford only wood rather than silver, the wood should be beautifully carved and polished. With daily rituals like hand-washing, a more elaborate jug might be kept for Shabbat and the festivals.

THE HOLY ARK AND TORAH SCROLLS

Inside the richly decorated Holy Ark are the holy Torah scrolls. They are usually protected with an embroidered curtain, as well as wooden doors and wrought-iron gates. You can see the embroidered curtain in the photograph, pulled back to the left. Those scrolls at the back of the Ark are sometimes old and not fit for use, but they are still treasured. Those that are used have silver breastplates, pointers and bells or crowns, as well as embroidered velvet covers.

SPICE BOXES

In the Havdalah ceremony at the end of Shabbat, a box of spices is passed around for each person to smell. This is to refresh the soul for the coming week. To make the ceremony even more special, the spice boxes are often beautifully decorated and designed as castles, windmills and towers. They are carved from wood or made of decorated silver, glass or china.

TORAH POINTERS

Pointers, used to mark the place while reading from the Torah, are often made of silver. The end is sometimes shaped like a fist with a finger pointing. Pointers are used because the Torah scroll must not be touched by hand.

Silver pointers

Noisemaker

NOISEMAKERS

When reading the story of Purim, Jews are commanded to blot out the name of the villain, Haman, whenever it is read out (see page 31). Noisemakers of all shapes and materials have been designed, some like football rattles!

Dreidls

SPINNING TOPS

The *dreidl*, or *sevivon*, is a spinning top for use on Chanukkah. It has four Hebrew letters, which stand for 'a Great Miracle Happened There'. Each letter is also an instruction to give or take counters in a game.

MARRIAGE CERTIFICATE

The *ketubah* – marriage certificate – not only sets out the details of the marriage, but also contains details of the money and goods the groom must give his bride if the marriage ends in divorce. Marriage certificates are often handwritten and beautifully decorated like the one above. They may be on display in the home.

THE ETERNAL LIGHT

The *Ner Tamid,* or Eternal Light, is found hanging from the ceiling of the synagogue. As you can see in the photograph on the right, it is directly in front of the Holy Ark. The light, inside its ornate container, burns all the time in many synagogues. With electricity this is no longer a problem! The Ner Tamid is a symbol of the menorah in the Temple, in which the purest olive oil was burned. It is also a reminder that the Torah is the guiding light of the Jews.

·DO·JEWS· ·HAVE·A· TRADITION ·OF·MUSIC- MAKING?

There is a very strong tradition of Jewish music-making. This is recorded as far back as the time of the Exodus from Egypt. There were musical instruments made especially for use in the Temple. In many Orthodox synagogues, musical instruments are never used on Shabbat or on festival days, the only music being singing. However, many Progressive synagogues do use musical instruments in their services. Folk-songs are found in every Jewish community. They are used to comfort, to entertain and to pass on history and traditions.

MIRIAM AND THE WOMEN

After the Israelites' miraculous escape from the pursuing Egyptians at the Red Sea, Moses composed a hymn to God. This is recorded in the Torah, for all to sing. Miriam took the women off separately to dance and sing the hymn, playing on her timbrel, as the painting shows. At many Orthodox weddings, it is still customary for women and men to dance and sing separately.

Timbrel

Trumpet

Cymbals

MUSIC IN THE TENAKH

In the *Tenakh*, many musical instruments are mentioned. Perhaps the most famous are: Miriam's timbrel – a type of tambourine; King David's lyre – a small harp; and the shofar – the ram's horn. The noise from the shofar brought down the walls of Jericho. When the Israelites were camped in the desert, silver trumpets were blown to call the tribes either to a meeting, or to march, or to war. Bugles are used in much the same way in modern armies. As well as harps and lyres, flutes, cymbals and trumpets were played in the Temple. Other instruments mentioned in the *Tenakh* are drums, bells and clappers or rattles.

WEDDING MUSIC

It is considered especially important to make the bride happy at her wedding. A Jewish wedding is not complete without its musicians. As well as special tunes for psalms and hymns, there are some hauntingly beautiful melodies composed especially for weddings. Today, the bride is often escorted to the wedding canopy with beautiful singing by a cantor or choir. At the celebratory meal, the couple are entertained with happy songs and instrumental tunes. A traditional group of musicians, known as *klezmer* musicians, used to provide the music in each town or village for special occasions.

Bells

Lyre

Shofar

FOLK-DANCING

There are many Jewish folk-dances. Some date from biblical times and use songs and poems from the *Tenakh*. Others are from countries in which Jews lived for centuries, such as Russia and the Arab lands. Sometimes they use Jewish dances and words, but the tunes come from the host countries. For Jews in many lands folk-dancing is popular as a hobby, at weddings and for all festive occasions, as you can see in the photograph on the right.

· DO · JEWS · HAVE · A · TRADITION · OF · STORY- TELLING ?

All of the laws and traditions of Judaism have been passed on down the generations through story-telling. At the Pesach Seder service, the whole family is expected to sit round the table. They tell and re-tell the story of the slavery of the Jews in Egypt, the Ten Plagues and the eventual Exodus from Egypt, as if each member of the family had personally left Egypt. The Torah itself, the rest of the *Tenakh* and the *Talmud* teach their historical, social, ethical and legal lessons largely through story-telling. The greatest Jewish teachers have often been those who could put over their lessons in dramatic or witty stories.

JONAH AND THE BIG FISH
The book of Jonah the Prophet, from the *Tenakh*, teaches repentance and forgiveness. Jonah refuses God's command to instruct the people of Nineveh (a Middle-Eastern city) to be sorry for their evil ways. He tries to escape from God by taking a ship to Spain. The ship is struck by a storm. Jonah, realising this is his punishment, insists on being thrown overboard. The storm stops and he is swallowed by an enormous fish (as shown in the painting). After praying to God, Jonah is thrown up on land and agrees to go to Nineveh. He persuades the people to repent and they are also forgiven by God.

SAYINGS AND PROVERBS

Throughout the *Tenakh*, the *Talmud* and many of the other Jewish holy books, there are many wise and witty sayings and proverbs that are still used today.

Here are just a few examples:

'Do not judge a man until you have stood in his place.'

'A fool says what he knows, a wise man knows what he says.'

'In the country of the blind, the one-eyed man is king.'

'Do not do to others what you would not like them to do to you.'

'God gave man one mouth and two ears so that he could listen twice as much as he could speak.'

42

RABBI AKIVA

Rabbi Akiva (50–135 CE) was one of the greatest rabbis of his time. Many of his rulings are given in the *Talmud*. There are also dozens of stories that he told, and which were told about him, to comfort and strengthen his followers during the time of Roman oppression in which they lived.

His own life story is a great romance. Starting life as a poor shepherd boy, Akiva ben Joseph fell in love with his wealthy master's daughter, Rachel. Although her father cast them out without a penny, Rachel insisted, as a condition of their marriage, that Akiva become a Torah scholar. They were so poor that Rachel had to sell her hair so that they could eat. However, they both heroically carried on with their intentions.

Eventually, Akiva became a great scholar and Rachel's father, ashamed of his lack of faith in his daughter, begged their forgiveness. Rabbi Akiva died a martyr's death. He was burned alive by the Romans for teaching the Torah. However, to the wonder of his followers, he died with great dignity and even joy. He said that he finally understood and could carry out the command of the Shema prayer – to love God with all his heart and soul.

CHILDREN LISTENING TO A STORY

These Jewish children are learning about Jewish traditions through listening to stories. The stories may be from the Torah, or they may be new stories. These help them to understand what being Jewish means to them.

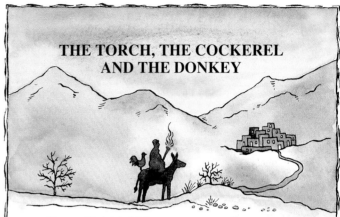

THE TORCH, THE COCKEREL AND THE DONKEY

Once, Rabbi Akiva went on a journey, riding on a donkey. He carried with him a cockerel to wake him in the morning and a torch of burning pitch to light his way in the dark. He finally came to a small village, but no one was willing to give him a bed for the night. Instead of being angry, he just shrugged his shoulders and said, 'Whatever is God's will is for the best', and he went out of the village to sleep in a field. During the night, a lion killed and carried off the donkey, a fox feasted on the cockerel, and a strong wind blew out the torch. He accepted each disaster as God's will.

Next morning, he awoke to find that the village had been attacked by armed robbers in the night. They had killed all the people and stolen their goods.

'I see now that all is in God's hand', he said to himself. 'Had the people been more hospitable, I would have stayed with them. Had my torch stayed alight, my donkey brayed or my cockerel crowed, the robbers would have found me, even in the field, and killed me too.'

·GLOSSARY·

BAR MITZVAH A Jewish boy who reaches the age of 13 is a Bar Mitzvah. This means he is considered a man in Jewish law. He must keep all the laws that apply to Jewish men.

BAT MITZVAH A Jewish girl who reaches the age of 12 is a Bat Mitzvah. This means that she is considered a woman in Jewish law, She must keep all the laws that apply to Jewish women.

CHANUKKAH The Feast of the Re-dedication of the Temple. It lasts for eight days. It begins on 25 *Kislev* and commemorates the events of 140–138 BCE.

CHASIDIC JEWS Jews who follow the branch of Judaism known as Chasidism. Each Chasidic group was founded by a leader, known as a Rebbe.

CIRCUMCISION The act of cutting off the loose skin at the tip of the penis known as the foreskin. It is a sign of the covenant Abraham made with God.

COVENANT In the *Tenakh*, a covenant is a solemn agreement between God and human beings. Usually, God gives a sign to show that he will keep his promise and the human beings do something important to show that they will keep their promise.

ISRAELITES The name given to the people who were descendants of Israel, as Jacob was later known. The name 'Jews' was adopted much later. The Israelites were permanently divided into twelve tribes for every activity. Each tribe consisted of the direct male descendants of one of Jacob's sons, plus their wives, families and servants. Each tribe had its own place to live and duties to carry out.

KIPPAH (or yarmulke) A small round cap that Jewish boys and men wear on top of their heads. Some only wear a kippah when praying, some wear it all day .

KOSHER Kosher food is food that the Torah lists as being suitable for Jews to eat. It includes any fruit and vegetables, cereals and other foods which grow in the ground or on trees and bushes. Only fish with fins and scales, such as cod, animals which eat grass and vegetables (and chew the cud) and have split hooves, such as cows, and a list of named birds, such as chickens, are permitted. Animals and birds must be killed in a special way called 'Shechitah' and all blood must be drained away before the flesh can be eaten.

MATZAH Unleavened bread, made only of flour and water, but no yeast. It is the bread that slaves used to eat in Egypt. It is flat and crispy.

MIKVEH A pool of 'living' water, from either rain, a river or the sea. Objects or people are completely dipped in mikveh water as a sign of religious purity.

PESACH The festival of freedom from slavery. In Israel it lasts for seven days and eight days outside Israel, beginning on 15 *Nisan*. It commemorates the Exodus of the Children of Israel from slavery in Egypt.

PURIM The Feast of Lots, celebrated each year on 14 *Adar*. Haman, the Persian Prime Minister, cast lots to see which was the best day for killing all the Jews in the Empire of King Xerxes II. The Jewish Queen, Esther, and Mordechai her uncle, exposed Haman. The Festival of Purim was established to mark the miraculous survival of the Jews.

ROSH HASHANAH The New Year, celebrated each year on 1 and 2 *Tishrei*. The Jewish New Year is a time for thinking about your actions of the past year, and making plans to improve yourself for the coming year.

SHABBAT The seventh day of Creation. On this day, God rested from doing any further work. In the fourth of the Ten Commandments, Jews are told to remember this day every week, to rest and keep it holy.

SHAVUOT The Festival of the First Fruits. It is also the Festival of the Giving of the Torah.

SUKKOT The Harvest Festival, celebrated for seven days. The eighth day is known as *Shemini Atzeret*.

TABERNACLE The Tabernacle was the magnificent tent of meeting, prayer and sacrifice which was made by the Israelites in the Wilderness, at God's command. It was the original home of the two stone tablets engraved with the Ten Commandments, located inside their precious golden box, the Ark. The Tabernacle was portable and was taken with the Israelites wherever they went. The Ark was always taken with the Israelites when they fought wars, to give them courage and strength.

TALLIT A prayer shawl with fringes at each of the four corners. Orthodox men wrap themselves in a prayer shawl for many prayer services. Progressive Jews permit both men and women to wear the tallit.

TALMUD That part of the Torah that was dictated to Moses at Sinai, but not meant to be written down. Eventually, the rabbis realised that it would be lost if not written down, and so the Talmud was written as a set of books.

TEFILLIN Tefillin are two small square boxes that contain the Shema prayer and other paragraphs from the Torah, attached to the head and arm by leather straps.

TEMPLE The first Temple was built by King Solomon, son of King David, to be the holiest place for prayers and sacrifices. It was where the two stone tablets engraved with the Ten Commandments inside the Holy Ark were housed. It was destroyed by the Greeks. A replacement was built which was later destroyed by the Romans. Orthodox Jews pray every day for the Temple to be rebuilt.

TORAH The first written part of the Jewish bible. It consists of the Five Books of Moses.

YOM KIPPUR The Day of Atonement, the most solemn festival. It is also a 25-hour fast.

· I N D E X ·